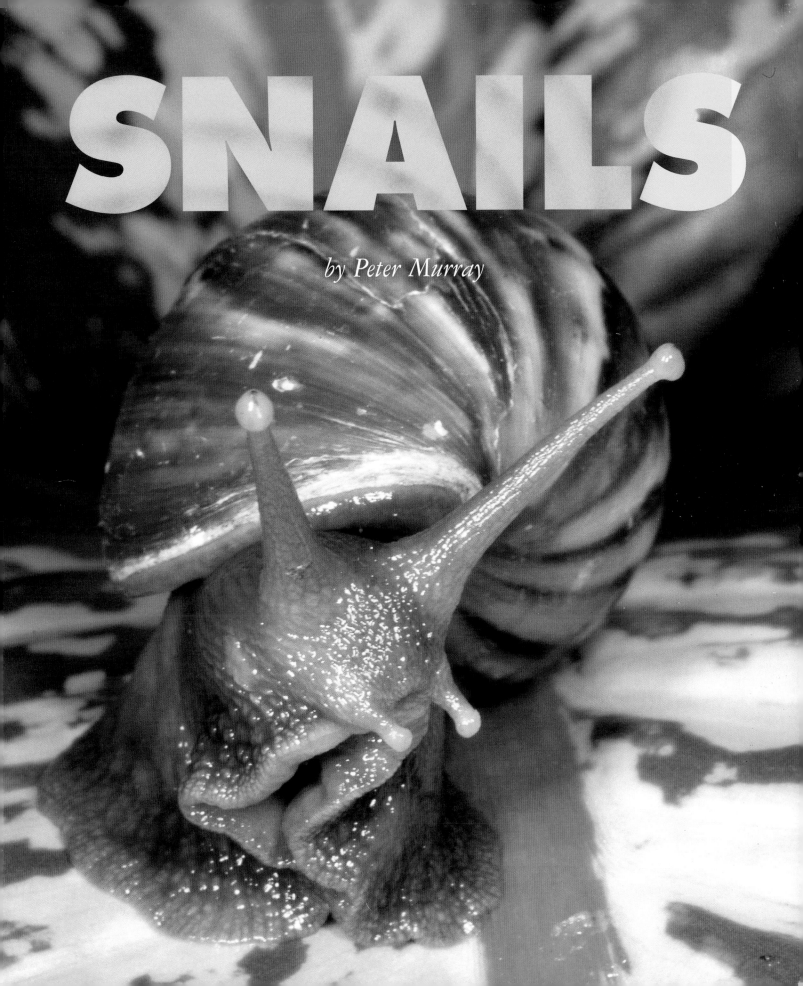

SNAILS

by Peter Murray

Content Adviser:
Winston Card,
Conservation Program
Manager, Cincinnati Zoo
& Botanical Garden

Published in the United States of America by The Child's World®
PO Box 326 • Chanhassen, MN 55317-0326
800-599-READ • www.childsworld.com

PHOTO CREDITS

© Alex Kerstitch/Visuals Unlimited: 22–23
© Arthur Morris/Corbis: 27
© Bruce Coleman, Inc./Alamy: 25
© David Fleetham/Alamy: 16–17
© Fred Whitehead/ Animals Animals-Earth Scenes: 13
© Gary Meszaros/Photo Researchers, Inc.: 10
© Imagebroker/Alamy: 20
© Karl Switak/Gallo Images/Corbis: 19
© Ken Wilson/Papilio/Corbis: 14–15
© Lance Nelson/Corbis: 28
© Lourens Smak/Alamy: 21
© Martin Harvey/Corbis: 11
© Oswald Eckstein/zefa/Corbis: 9
© Peter Steiner/Corbis: 6–7
© Richard Shiell/Dembinsky Photo Associates: 5
© Robert and Linda Mitchell: cover, 1

ACKNOWLEDGMENTS

The Child's World®: Mary Berendes, Publishing Director;
Katherine Stevenson, Editor

The Design Lab: Kathleen Petelinsek, Design and Page Production

LIBRARY OF CONGRESS CATALOGING-IN-PUBLICATION DATA

Murray, Peter, 1952 Sept. 29–
  Snails / by Peter Murray.
    p. cm. — (New naturebooks)
  Includes bibliographical references and index.
  ISBN 1-59296-650-0 (library bound : alk. paper)
  1. Snails—Juvenile literature. I. Title. II. Series.
  QL430.4.M892 2006
  594'.3—dc22   2006001377

Table of Contents

On the cover: A giant African snail like this one can grow up to 12 inches (30 cm) long—and that's not including its shell! Because these huge snails eat many types of plants, fruits, and vegetables, many farmers consider them to be pests.

Meet the Snail!

Snails have been around since about 600 million years ago—long before the first dinosaurs.

Early one summer morning, you're looking at your family's vegetable garden. Dewdrops on the tomato plants sparkle in the sunlight. You notice something very small moving on one of the leaves. You step closer and see a small, legless animal creeping along. It seems to have some kind of shell on its back! As you watch, it crawls slowly across the leaf, leaving a shiny trail behind it. What is this strange little animal? It's a snail!

This common garden snail is creeping along a leaf on a cloudy day. Can you guess how garden snails got their name?

What Are Snails?

Gastropods are the only mollusks that have adapted to living on land.

Snails belong to a large group of animals called **mollusks**. There are thousands of different kinds of mollusks. They include snails, slugs, squid, octopuses, and clams. Mollusks have soft bodies with no backbone. Many mollusks have a shell on the outside, and some have a shell on the inside. Others have no shell at all. Many mollusks also have a single muscular foot for moving around.

Snails and slugs are both *gastropods*, which make up a large part of the mollusk group. Snails usually have a shell on the outside of their body, eyes, a mouth, and **tentacles** for feeling, tasting, and smelling the things around them. Slugs are a lot like snails, but they usually don't have a shell.

You can see this grove snail's soft body and tentacles as it leans over the edge of a rock. Grove snails are common in Europe.

What Do Snails Look Like?

The eyes of most land snails are at the ends of their longer tentacles. The eyes of most water snails are at the bottom of the tentacles, near the head.

If a snail's shell gets damaged, the snail can usually repair it.

The shells of some snails coil to the right, while the shells of others coil to the left.

Except for their hard shells, snails are soft and slimy. Their heads usually have two pairs of tentacles and one pair of eyes. A snail's mouth usually faces downward toward the ground. Snails can't hear—they don't have any ears.

The snail's shell is made by and connected to the snail's body. The snail can't leave its shell, but it can push most of its body out of the opening. The shell spirals toward one side of the snail's body. Some snail shells have a flatter spiral, and others are more pointed. The snail can pull itself inside through the shell's large opening. Many snails can close the opening with a "door" called an *operculum* (oh-PER-kyuh-lum).

This Roman snail is creeping up a twig. You can see its round eyes at the top of its tentacles.

Here you can see a colorful bunch of shells from sea snails.

Snail shells come in different colors. Most land snails and freshwater snails are brown, tan, green, or olive, sometimes with markings. These colors and markings help the snails blend in with their surroundings. Some ocean snails are especially colorful and have beautiful patterns on their shells.

Some snails are as tiny as the head of a pin. Others are as big as a golf ball. Some types of snails grow even bigger. The biggest land snail ever recorded was a giant African snail almost 15 inches (38 cm) long and weighing two pounds (almost 1 kg)! The biggest freshwater snail is a giant apple snail, which has a round shell up to 6 inches (15 cm) across. The largest sea snail is the Australian trumpet. The biggest Australian trumpet ever found was almost 31 inches (78 cm) long and weighed nearly 40 pounds (18 kg)!

This picture shows dozens of shells from land snails.

People sometimes find the shells of sea snails washed up on the beach. Collecting these beautiful shells can be a lot of fun.

Some snail shells are beautiful on the inside, too. Abalones are the source of colorful mother-of-pearl used for making jewelry and other items.

11

Where Do Snails Live?

It's amazing that anything can live by hot vents in the sea floor. The water from these vents is superheated deep inside the earth and comes out as hot as 752°F (400°C)—four times hotter than boiling water!

Ocean snails tend to have thicker shells than land snails. The thick shells protect them from enemies, and the water helps support the added weight.

Snails live all over the world. Many types of snails live on land. They live in all different kinds of areas—rain forests, grassy plains, mountainous regions, and even deserts. Other types of snails live in freshwater rivers, lakes, or streams. Still others live in the ocean. Some ocean snails make their homes near the shore. Others live deeper on the ocean floor, on coral reefs, and even in the freezing waters of the Arctic and Antarctic. A few snails even live by hot vents on the ocean's floor.

Periwinkles live in ocean beach areas that are underwater when the water is high and exposed to the air when the water is low. When they are out of the water, periwinkles glue their shell edges to the rocks to keep from drying out.

Most land snails don't like freezing temperatures. They don't like bright sunlight or hot, dry weather, which can kill them by drying them out. They prefer places that are cool, shady, and moist, and they're most active at night or on cloudy days. Land snails that must survive very cold weather **hibernate**, or slow down their bodies, until the weather warms up again. When they hibernate, they use very little energy to stay alive.

Land snails that must survive very hot, dry weather **estivate**. Estivation is like hibernation, except that the snail uses **mucus** to seal itself inside its shell, to save water instead of energy. Some snails can estivate for days, months, or even years.

This garden snail has sealed itself inside its shell. Why do you think it's done that?

Snails are an important part of their natural surroundings. But if they get loose in places where they don't belong, they can cause big problems for other plants and animals. One Florida boy brought home three giant African snails from Hawaiʻi. His grandmother turned them loose in her garden. A few years later, there were over 18,000 of these huge pests!

15

What's Inside a Snail's Body?

Most crabs have their own outer shells. Hermit crabs, however, slip their soft bodies into old, abandoned snail shells and carry them around. When they outgrow one shell, they find another.

A snail's body isn't like yours. You have bones to support and protect your body. A snail's body is soft and squishy. Its outer shell gives it support and protection and keeps it from drying out.

Inside the snail's soft body are its heart, its brain, and its **digestive system** for breaking down food. These systems are much simpler than yours. Many land snails have a single lung. The lung allows them to get their oxygen from the air, just as you do. Some snails that live in the water have **gills** instead of a lung. These snails use their gills to get oxygen directly from the water, like fish. Other water snails have lungs but must come out of the water to breathe air.

Horse conchs (KONKS) like this one can be huge—their shells can be up to 24 inches (61 cm) long! These big sea snails move slowly along the ocean floor searching for other mollusks to eat.

How Do Snails Move?

The fastest land snails are garden snails, which move up to 165 feet (50 m) per hour. Some land snails move only about 23 inches (58 cm) per hour.

A snail's mucus also helps protect it. In fact, a snail can crawl over the edge of a razor blade without getting hurt!

People have two feet. Cats and dogs have four. Insects have six. But snails have only one "foot." In fact, the word gastropod means "stomach foot." Why did people give snails and slugs this name? Because it looks as though these animals are walking around on their bellies.

To move around more easily, land snails make slippery trails. They put out a slick, slimy mucus on their foot. Wavelike movements in the foot pull the snail slowly along the trail of slime. Some water snails use their foot to pull themselves along. A few are able to swim.

This giant African snail is making its way across a rock in South Africa's Kruger National Park. You can see the trail of slime it's leaving behind.

What Do Snails Eat?

Like you, snails need minerals to make their bodies strong. Sometimes they use their radula to grind away bits of rock or bone to get calcium for building their shells.

Wolf snails track down other snails and eat them. Their long lips taste the slime trail the other snails leave behind.

Different snails eat different kinds of things. Most snails have a raspy tongue called a *radula* that is covered with thousands of tiny teeth. Snails use their radula to scrape up food. The teeth are constantly wearing away and being replaced.

Many land snails eat plant foods such as fresh green leaves, tender young shoots, flowers, fruits, and vegetables. That's why many gardeners think of them as pests! Other land snails eat dead leaves and dead animals. These snails help the plant and animal matter break down, or **decompose**, so that it becomes part of the soil. Some snails eat mostly earthworms. Some even eat other snails!

20

On this page you can see the radula of an apple snail. The facing page shows a hungry garden snail as it feeds on a flower bud.

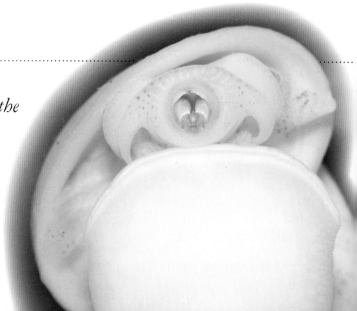

Many snails that live in water eat plants, too. Some sea snails eat seaweed and algae (AL-gee). Others feed on plant and animal matter that settles to the bottom. Some are meat-eaters that feed on starfish, sand dollars, and mollusks such as clams and oysters. Moon snails, drupes, and drills are all snails that drill right through the shells of other mollusks, then suck out the insides.

Did you know that there are poisonous snails? Cone snails live in the ocean and hunt worms, other mollusks, or fish. They stab these animals with their needle-like *proboscis* (pro-BOSS-kiss) and shoot in a substance that makes the animals unable to move. The cone snails then eat the helpless animals. Cone snails' poison can even be dangerous to humans.

Here you can see a cone snail as it swallows a fish off the coast of Mexico.

A cone snail's proboscis is a single radula tooth that shoots out like a harpoon, carrying poison. Cone-snail poisons have been used to make medicines for treating pain.

The Atlantic oyster drill is a snail that kills large numbers of oysters. Oyster drills use their radulas and acid to make a hole all the way through the oyster's shell.

23

What Are Baby Snails Like?

Common garden snails' eggs are the size of BBs.

The eggs of a giant African snail are an inch (2.5 cm) across— larger than many other kinds of adult snails!

On snails that aren't fully grown, the shell opening has sharp edges. When the snails become adults, the opening has a more rounded, thicker edge.

Snails hatch from eggs. The eggs must be **fertilized** before they can grow into babies. In some snail species, the snails are either male or female. The male fertilizes the eggs, and the female lays them in a safe place. In other species, the snails are both male and female. These **hermaphrodites** have both male and female body parts. When these snails mate, they fertilize the eggs inside each other's bodies. Some can even fertilize their own eggs!

Some land snails dig holes for their eggs. Others lay them under rocks or dead leaves. Sea and freshwater snails usually lay their soft eggs in a jellylike mass.

Some baby snails are born with their shell, and some are not. As the snail grows, it adds new shell only at the opening. The middle of the spiral is the oldest, and the part nearest the opening is the newest.

This apple snail is laying its eggs on a reed near a Florida pond. By laying their eggs above the water, these snails keep the eggs safe from fish and other water-dwelling enemies.

Do Snails Have Enemies?

People eat snails, too. Large land snails are raised on farms and served as escargot (ess-kar-GOH) in restaurants all over the world. People also eat several kinds of sea snails, including abalone, conch, and periwinkle.

Some land snails produce a foamy mucus to protect themselves from small insects such as ants.

Lots of animals eat snails, including lizards, insects, birds, fish, frogs and toads, salamanders, and even other snails. Snail kites are birds that eat almost nothing but freshwater apple snails. They use their hooked beak to tear the snail from its shell. Another animal that eats snails is the firefly **larva**. The larva shoots a poison into the snail, then eats it.

People are one of snails' biggest enemies. People use poisons to kill land snails that eat garden crops. They sometimes kill sea snails for their beautiful shells. They also kill snails accidentally, by destroying or dirtying areas where the snails live. Some types of snails have become quite rare. In some countries, governments have passed laws to protect certain kinds of snails.

This hungry snail kite has found an apple snail to eat. Snail kites will also eat crabs, turtles, and mice, but snails are by far their favorite meal.

26

Sometimes snails can be pests, such as when they eat crops or get loose in places where they don't belong. But in the right places, snails are an important part of our natural world. They provide food for many types of animals and help to break down dead plant and animal matter.

No matter where you are, there are probably snails living close to you. Try looking for them at night or early in the morning. Sometimes you can also find them after a gentle rain. Check under logs or old boards or in piles of dead leaves. If you look hard enough, you will probably find a snail!

Snails are easily affected by changes in the air, water, and soil—including pollution.

Many snails can live to be about five years old, but some can live up to 15 years.

In some parts of the world, conch shells have been used like trumpets.

This boy is getting a close-up view of a garden snail. After studying the snail for a little while, he put it right back on the leaf where he found it.

Glossary

decompose (dee-kum-POHZ) To decompose is to rot, or to break down into simpler parts. Snails help plant and animal matter decompose.

digestive system (dy-JES-tiv SIS-tum) An animal's digestive system includes the organs and substances used to break food down into smaller pieces the body can use. A snail's digestive system is within the part of its body that is always inside the shell.

estivate (ESS-ti-vayt) To estivate is to go into an inactive state for the summer or during hot, dry weather. Some land snails estivate.

fertilized (FUR-tuh-lyzed) When an egg is fertilized, it begins to grow into a baby animal. Some snails fertilize their own eggs.

gills (GILZ) Gills are organs on some animals that allow the animals to breathe underwater. Some water snails have gills.

hermaphrodites (her-MAF-ruh-dyts) Hermaphrodites are animals or plants with both male and female body parts. Some snails are hermaphrodites.

hibernate (HY-bur-nayt) To hibernate is to go into a very deep sleep, to save energy and survive through the winter. Some land snails hibernate.

larva (LAR-vuh) In some animals, a larva is the young, very different form of the animal when it first hatches or is born. The larva goes through big changes before it becomes an adult. Firefly larvae eat snails.

mollusks (MAH-lusks) Mollusks are soft, boneless animals that often have an inside or outside shell and one foot for moving around. Snails are mollusks.

mucus (MYOO-kuss) Mucus is a wet slime produced by some animals' bodies. A snail's skin is covered in slimy mucus.

tentacles (TEN-ti-kulz) Tentacles are long, bendable body parts that some animals use for touching and sensing things around them. A snail's eyes are on its tentacles.

To Find Out More

Read It!

Buholzer, Theres. *Life of the Snail.* Minneapolis, MN: Carolrhoda Books, 1987.

Coldry, Jennifer. *Discovering Slugs and Snails.* New York: Bookwright Press, 1987.

Gilpin, Daniel. *Snails, Shellfish, & Other Mollusks.* Minneapolis, MN: Compass Point Books, 2006.

Johnson, Sylvia A. *Snails.* Minneapolis, MN: Lerner Publishing, 1982.

Llewellyn, Claire, and Barrie Watts (photographer). *Slugs and Snails.* Danbury, CT: Franklin Watts, 2002.

Pascoe, Elaine, and Dwight Kuhn (photographer). *Slugs and Snails.* Woodbridge, CT: Blackbirch Press, 1999.

Ross, Michael Elsohn. *Snailology.* Minneapolis, MN: Carolrhoda Books, 1996.

Watts, Barrie. *Snail.* Danbury, CT: Franklin Watts, 2005.

On the Web

Visit our home page for lots of links about snails:
http://www.childsworld.com/links

Note to Parents, Teachers, and Librarians: We routinely check our Web links to make sure they're safe, active sites—so encourage your readers to check them out!

Index